EARTHQUAKE

BY **Milly Lee**

PICTURES BY **Yangsook Choi**

FRANCES FOSTER BOOKS • FARRAR, STRAUS AND GIROUX

NEW YORK

Distributed in Canada by Douglas & McIntyre Ltd.
Color separations by Chroma Graphics
Printed and bound in the United States of America
by Worzalla
Typography by Judy Lanfredi
First edition, 2001
10 9 8 7 6 5 4 3 2 1

Library of Congress Cataloging-in-Publication Data
Lee, Milly.
    Earthquake / Milly Lee ; pictures by Yangsook Choi.— 1st ed.
      p. cm.
    Summary: A young Chinese-American girl and her family move their belongings from their home in Chinatown
to the safety of Golden Gate Park during the San Francisco earthquake of 1906.
      ISBN 0-374-39964-6
    1. Earthquakes—California—San Francisco—Juvenile fiction. [1. Earthquakes—California—San Francisco—
Fiction. 2. Chinese-Americans—Fiction. 3. San Francisco (Calif.)—Fiction.] I. Choi, Yangsook, ill. II. Title.

PZ7.L51433 Ear 2001
[E]—dc21
                                                                                    00-26213

For Ed, Gwen, Ivy, and Virginia
and in memory of Florence and our parents, Henry and Lillian Chan —M.L.

For Frances —Y.C.

This morning the earth shook
and threw us from our beds.
We were not hurt, just stunned.

Drawers spilled, dishes crashed,
pots and pans clanged as they fell.
Ancestral portraits flew off the walls.

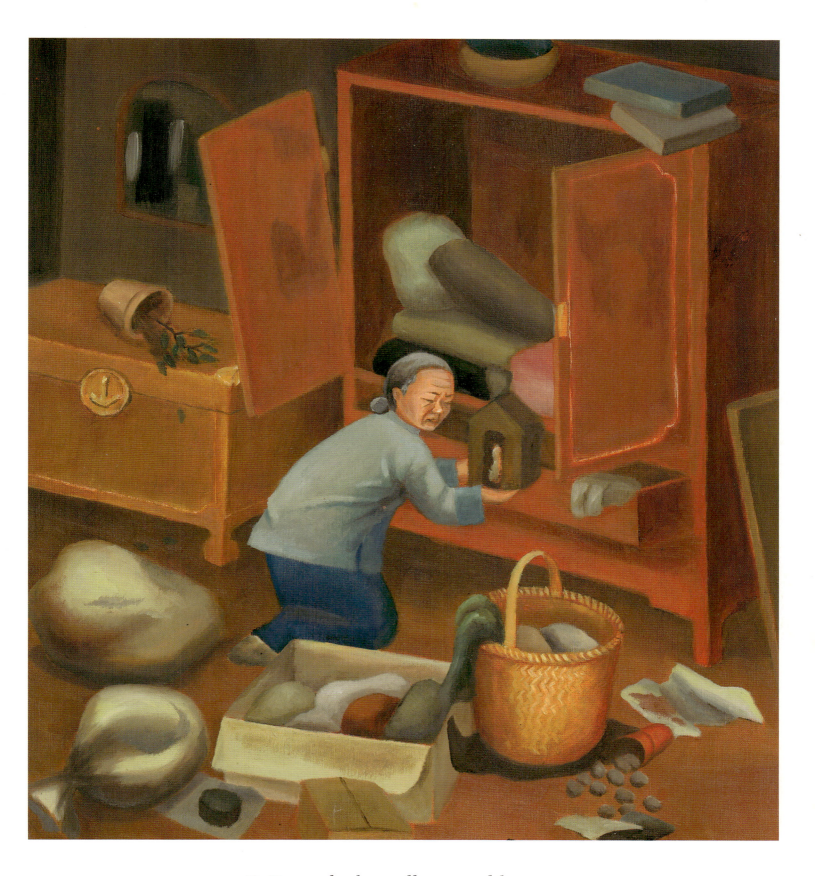

PoPo packed up all we could carry—
bedding, clothing, food, utensils;
Kwan Yin and ancestors, too.

MaMa told us to hurry,
wear extra layers of clothes,
and prepare to leave for safety.

BaBa hurried out to seek help
and returned with a cart
and two kinsmen.

Carefully and slowly
we made our way down the stairs
to load the cart with our belongings.

In the early dawn, confused and frightened,
we gathered at Portsmouth Square.
All of Chinatown must have been there.

"You must go to Golden Gate Park!"
shouted the policeman.
"The city is on fire. Go quickly now!"

Dark smoke hurt our eyes.
Gritty dust filled the air,
our mouths and noses, too.

The earth shook again.
We stopped, and watched in fear
as buildings crumbled around us.

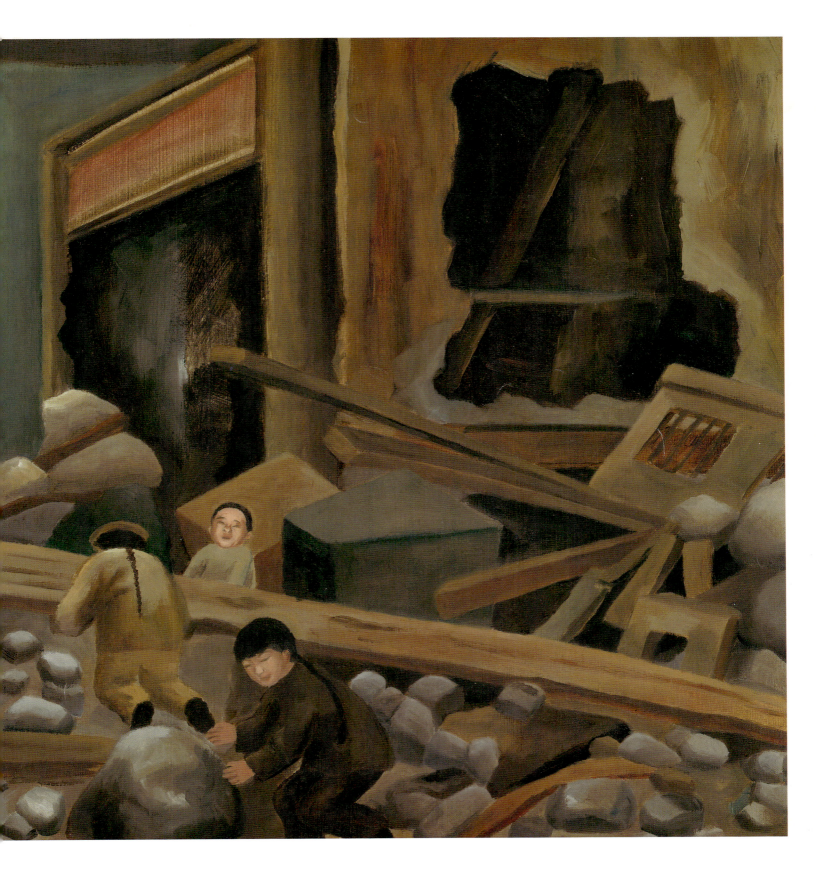

Elder Brother, Younger Brother, and I
cleared a path for the cart carrying
MaMa and PoPo and our belongings.

We were hot and thirsty
until we shed the extra clothing
and drank some cold tea.

In the early-morning rush to leave,
we had not eaten anything.
PoPo gave us crackers and dried fruit.

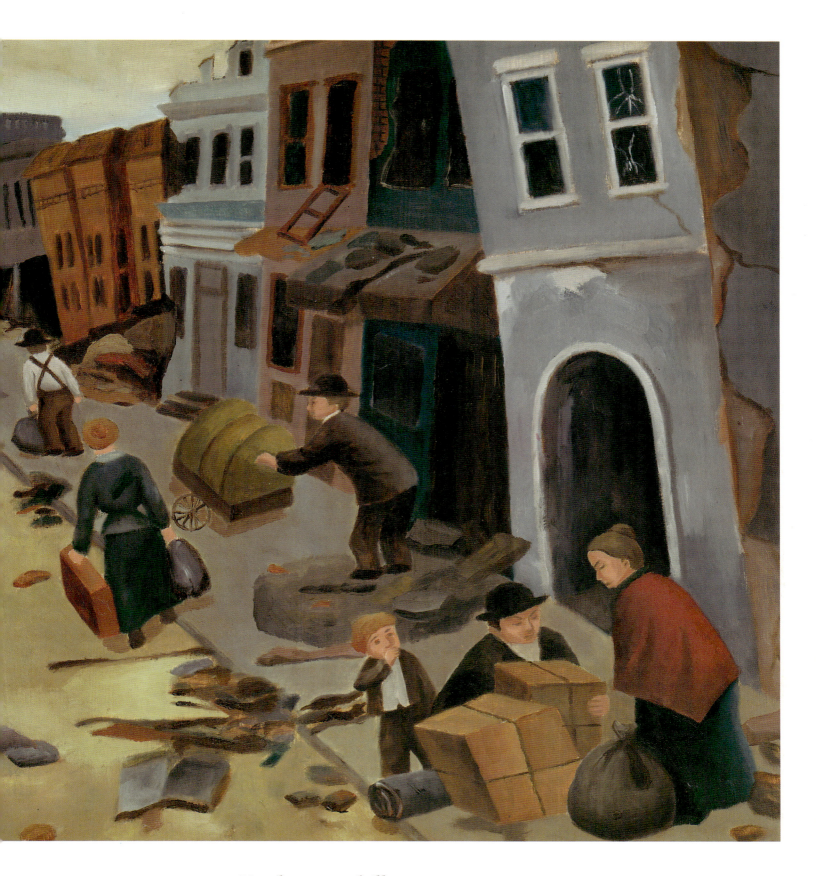

Up the steep hills,
across the city,
we pushed and pulled the heavy cart.

All around us, frightened people
struggled with loads
too dear to leave behind.

Terrified dogs, cats,
and horses joined the people
hurrying to safety.

Until, at last, we were away
from the spreading fires.
Away from falling buildings.

In Golden Gate Park
there was food, water,
and tents for shelter.

PoPo, BaBa, MaMa,
Elder Brother, Younger Brother, and I
rested and ate.

We were safe for now
while the city still burned
and the earth still shook.

AUTHOR'S NOTE

On Wednesday, April 18, 1906, at 5:13 a.m., an earthquake on the San Andreas Fault, measuring about 8.2 on the Richter scale, shook San Francisco. Buildings collapsed, and exploding gas mains caused widespread fires that could not be put out because water pipes were broken and it was difficult to move fire-fighting equipment through the rubble.

The city burned for more than three days, and most of San Francisco was destroyed. Although 478 deaths were reported, historians now say that more than 3,000 people died in the earthquake and fire. The original count had been taken from voter registration and property ownership lists, but those lists did not include women and children, Native Americans, African Americans, or Japanese and Chinese immigrants because they were not allowed to vote or own property at that time.

This is the story of one family on that fateful day, as told by a young Chinese American girl—my mother. Her family consisted of PoPo (her grandmother), BaBa (her father), MaMa (her mother), and two brothers. The family left their home in Chinatown to travel across town to Golden Gate Park, where they sought refuge in a tent city built by soldiers within hours of the first shock. The journey was especially difficult because PoPo and MaMa's feet had been bound when they were children, leaving them unable to walk for any length of time.

Like the portraits of ancestors, the statue of Kwan Yin, Goddess of Mercy, that stood on the family altar was not left behind when the family fled. The Buddhist deity, known for her compassion, was especially loved by women who sought her help in times of trouble.

After the fire, the family moved across the bay to Oakland's Chinatown, where they stayed for many months while San Francisco was being rebuilt.

Like the mythical phoenix, a magnificent new city rose from the rubble.